Harry Laurenz Wells

The war in the Philippines

Harry Laurenz Wells

The war in the Philippines

ISBN/EAN: 9783743323384

Manufactured in Europe, USA, Canada, Australia, Japa

Cover: Foto ©ninafisch / pixelio.de

Manufactured and distributed by brebook publishing software (www.brebook.com)

Harry Laurenz Wells

The war in the Philippines

THE WAR IN THE PHILIPPINES

BY

HARRY L. WELLS

CAPTAIN SECOND OREGON UNITED STATES VOLUNTEERS

AND SPECIAL WAR CORRESPONDENT
OF THE NEW YORK EVENING POST, ST. LOUIS GLOBE-DEMOCRAT
AND CHICAGO CHRONICLE

ILLUSTRATIONS FROM PHOTOGRAPHS TAKEN IN THE FIELD BY BREVET-MAJOR J. F. CASE
SECOND OREGON UNITED STATES VOLUNTEERS

SUNSET
PHOTOGRAVURE PRINTERS, PUBLISHERS
SAN FRANCISCO, CAL.

THE WAR IN THE PHILIPPINES

San Juan del Monte Bridge, showing Filipino Outpost, where Wm. Grayson of the First Nebraska fired the first shot of the Filipino War, February 4, 1899

American Occupation of Manila.

When Manila surrendered, on the thirteenth day of August, 1898, the American troops occupied the city, while the Filipino soldiers took up positions in the immediate outskirts. This left the line of Spanish defenses of the city in the hands of the Filipinos, the city being entirely undefended as against an attack by the natives, except by the valor of the troops occupying it. During the six months which elapsed before the breaking out of the rebellion, Aguinaldo busied himself enrolling a large army, estimated at 70,000 men, drilling them as much as possible, and building an elaborate system of entrenchments completely surrounding the city. The entire country outside of Manila came under his control, including the only railroad, and he was enabled to import without hindrance large quantities of arms and ammunition, since all seaports except Manila were left open to him. A careful investigation by a special officer resulted in the report that the Filipino army had about 40,000 guns, and that the remainder were armed with the bolo, a long, heavy bladed knife.

In contrast with this activity on the part of the natives was the carelessness and lack of preparation by the Americans. The army performed police duty, maintained outposts between the city and the Filipino positions, and did the usual amount of daily drill, but no special preparations seemed to have been made to carry on the warfare which nearly every man in the Philippines believed was almost certain to come. During the month of January, immediately following the issuance of the proclamation of sovereignty by the United States and counter proclamations by Aguinaldo, the relations were very strained and the utmost vigilance was exercised by the American forces. There were several false alarms, both in the daytime and at night, and in such instances the American troops were under arms and the entire city covered by them within ten minutes from the giving of the alarm; and without doubt this celerity and display of force so strongly impressed the native inhabitants of the city that when the outbreak finally occurred, they were afraid to undertake the general uprising which had been counted upon by Aguinaldo as the most important feature of his plan of attack upon the city.

Filipino Attack upon the City.

For a whole week before the fight began the Americans were warned that the Filipinos would attack them the following Sunday, and consequently were extremely alert and vigilant. However, hostilities began unexpectedly on Saturday night, and were undoubtedly prematurely precipitated, though the vigor with which the attack was taken up by the Filipinos along the entire line showed that they were ready for the

Block House No. 11 showing Guns and Filipino Flags Captured, February 5, by General King's Brigade.

battle and were pursuing a well concerted plan of operations. The first shot was fired by the outpost maintained by the Nebraska regiment at the San Juan del Monte bridge, by William Grayson. There had been several efforts made by Filipino officers to establish posts within our recognized lines, and on this occasion Filipinos approaching within our lines refused to halt when so ordered by the sentinel, who fired and probably killed the officer. His companion also fired immediately afterwards, and both were at once fired upon by a small body of Filipinos that had stolen up secretly to within a short distance of their post. This was shortly after eight o'clock in the evening. In a little while the attack was taken up by the Filipinos along the entire Nebraska front, and before ten o'clock had spread almost around the city.

Defeat of Aguinaldo's Army.

As soon as the alarm was given the American troops were immediately under arms and took the positions assigned to them. Some occupied positions of vantage about the city to quell any uprising, and others hastened to the outskirts to prevent the enemy from entering. The fight continued, with occasional lulls, throughout the entire night, the Americans remaining strictly on the defensive, only firing sufficiently to prevent the Filipinos from advancing, while the enemy poured in a heavy fire on all sides, wasting thousands of rounds of ammunition in the dark. When morning came the insurrectos had gained nothing, and up to that time our losses had been very light. During the night intelligence of the attack on the city was flashed to the fleet at Cavite by the patrol ships off Manila by search light signals cast on the sky, and the ships in the same way received their orders to aid in the counter attack that was being planned to take place at daylight. In the morning the American troops advanced and drove the Filipinos from their positions all along the line. This was undoubtedly a great surprise to them, accustomed as they had been, in fighting with the Spaniards, to make their attacks solely under cover of darkness and keep out of sight in the daytime. The Filipinos resisted the first attack with considerable stubbornness, apparently not realizing that the Americans would continue to advance in spite of the terrific fire and actually charge their breastworks. The result of this resistance was seen when the Americans passed over their lines, in the heaps of dead and wounded that lay in their trenches and along the ground immediately to their rear, the latter being shot while fleeing in terror before the line of blue and brown advancing with cheers and yells.

Troops Engaged

The troops engaged in this onslaught upon the Filipino intrenchments in the district between the Pasig river and the bay south of the city were the Washingtons, Idahos, Californias, one battalion of the Third

A Trench near Santa Ana after General King's Brigade had passed over it February 5

Artillery, acting as infantry, the North Dakotas, the Tennessees, the Fourteenth Regulars and a portion of the Sixth Artillery, and they were aided somewhat by vessels of the fleet, which shelled the intrenchments and woods back of them wherever practicable. On the north side of the river, clear around to the bay on the north of town, the troops engaged were the Nebraskas, Wyomings, Colorados, Pennsylvanias, South Dakotas, Montanas and Kansans, aided by the Utah Battery. The heaviest fighting on the south line was in the vicinity of Santa Ana, San Pedro Macati and Singalon. Near the latter place the Fourteenth Infantry lost heavily, Lieutenant Mitchell being among the killed. Colonel Smith of the Tennessees fell dead from his horse with apoplexy just as his regiment was deploying for the fight. Major McConville of the Idahos was killed while charging an insurgent battery. The fight at the latter point was particularly heavy, and the insurgent defense of this battery, which consisted of two Krupp field guns, was extremely stubborn. More of their dead were found on the ground at this place than at any other point on the line. The Californias, Idahos and Washingtons fought in this part of the field. On the north side of the river the heaviest fighting was in the vicinity of the Chinese cemetery, and was participated in by the Pennsylvanias, Montanas, Kansans and the Utah Battery. The next day the advance on the water works was made by the Nebraskas, Tennessees and the Oregons.

During all this time the city was constantly patrolled by the Minnesotas, Oregons and the Twenty-third Regulars, whose task was neither a pleasant one nor free from danger. They carried on a bushwhacking warfare with natives, who were in the swamps and bamboo thickets that abound within the city limits to the rear of our firing line, and who were firing upon our ambulances and persons going to and from the front. Their vigilance and activity nipped in the bud and thus cut off from the enemy the aid which they had counted upon to demoralize the Americans and render the capture of the city possible. At the end of the day's fighting new lines were established by the American forces and intrenchments thrown up, and they never again retired to their old positions.

Topography of Manila's Suburbs.

Manila lies on the seashore almost at the water level. The sloughs and creeks penetrate the city limits almost up to the walls of the old citadel, and the city straggles out in long rows of native huts on higher ground lying between them. These sloughs had to be crossed by our men in the face of terrific fire from the enemy concealed in bamboo thickets, protected by splendid breast works, and whose positions could

End of the Filipino Trench at Singalon, near which Lieutenant Mitchell of the Fourteenth Regulars was killed February 5.

not be accurately defined because the smokeless powder used gave no cloud of smoke to reveal their exact locality. The whole country around Manila is a region of rice fields interspersed with ditches, many of them crowned with rows of bamboo thickets, affording the finest kind of natural defense, so that the advance of our troops, even after the Filipino breastworks had been captured, was a continuous movement against these natural intrenchments occupied by a concealed enemy. The fact that our troops did advance under such circumstances and could not be stopped by the heaviest fire, so completely demoralized the Filipinos that never again during the entire war did they have the confidence in themselves which they possessed when they began the struggle. They seemed to realize from that time on that it was impossible for them to resist a determined attack on our part, and they never again stood up against the rush of our lines as they did when the first attack was made that Sunday morning. This demoralization increased as the war went on, until the Filipinos adopted the style of warfare which they are now pursuing, that of firing upon us at long range from concealed positions and abandoning them upon our approach for still other vantage points farther back.

Filipino Intrenchments around Manila.
The Filipino intrenchments were of the most elaborate and scientific construction. In places they were three rows deep, with connecting passages, so that the defenders might pass safely from one to another, and some of them were very cunningly constructed with a view of sweeping the first line of intrenchments with the fire from the others, after the first had been captured by our troops. In this, however, they were sorely disappointed, since the advance of our men was so swift and resistless that they were given no time to carry their well laid plans into execution. Not only was there this elaborate system of intrenchments, but smaller trenches and rifle pits covered all the approaches by the highways, and these were most cunningly concealed by the use of banana leaves, bamboo branches, etc. Little stone barricades were constructed under houses and sharpshooters were posted in them, so that our men received a fire from most unexpected sources, and it became necessary, as a matter of precaution, in advancing to fire into every house and clump of trees and at every object that looked in the least suspicious. The difficulty of locating the whereabouts of these little rifle pits was enhanced by the use of smokeless powder and the fact that the report made by the Mauser rifle is so deceptive that it seems utterly impossible to locate the position of a shooter by the report of a gun. To the other natural defenses were added the stone walls and the large stone churches, which were

Firing Line of the Twentieth Kansas in the Advance on Caloocan, February 10, near Block House No. 1.

occupied by the insurrectos. The better class of houses in Manila and suburbs and throughout the towns of the Island are surrounded with stone fences, and the houses themselves have the first story constructed of stone or cement. These were used as breastworks and forts by the natives, and had to be successively attacked and captured by our troops as they advanced. The church at Pāco was occupied by sharpshooters long after our main line had advanced beyond it, and they fired upon our wounded as they were being carried to the rear, and were only dislodged when the Sixth Artillery put a number of shells into the church which set it on fire. Even after that some sharpshooters got into the tower and remained there until the tower was practically demolished by the artillery. On the north side of the city the stone walls of the Chinese cemetery and the La Loma chapel constituted a strong fort, which required severe fighting for its capture.

For several days the American forces busied themselves in establishing permanent lines for the protection of the water works and for holding the insurgents in check on the south from San Pedro Macati to Malate, and on the tenth of February advance was made on the north to establish a new line from Caloocan to the water works. This movement was made by the Kansans, Montanas, Idahos, Third Artillery and Utah Battery, who drove the enemy from the Tondo district through a most difficult country of swamps and bamboo thickets clear through the town of Caloocan and back to the Tuliahan river, and established a new line beginning at the bayous fronting Malabon and passing around north of Caloocan and La Loma on to the extreme eastern end of the American lines at the Santolan pumping station. The fighting in this battle was extremely severe, and it was here that Lieutenant-Colonel Wallace, of the Montanas, was wounded. Caloocan was burned by the natives before they abandoned it, the only buildings left being the church, which had suffered somewhat from the artillery fire, a building which had been used by General Garcia as his headquarters, and the railroad station and engine shed. At this point was captured a large cannon which the natives had placed in position to bear down the railroad track, but which they did not use during the fight. It was an old style gun which had been brought over from the Spanish defenses of Cavite, and it is probable that the natives did not possess suitable ammunition for it. It still stands there beside the track as a monument to wasted energy. The Americans established new lines and threw up intrenchments facing Malabon and the river, continuing to Santolan, which were occupied by the Kansans, two guns of the Sixth Artillery, Montanas, one battalion of the Third Artillery as infantry, Pennsylvania, South Dakotas,

Battle of Caloocan.

Tondo Burned District. (See page 17.)

Colorados, one battalion of the Oregons and the Nebraskas. The Wyomings were stationed between this line and the Pasig river. The south line was held by the Washingtons, Californias, Idahos, Fourth Cavalry dismounted, and the Fourteenth Regulars. The Minnesotas, Oregons and the Twenty-third Regulars constituted the provost guard, the Iowas, Nevada Cavalry and California and Wyoming Artillery were at Cavite, and the Tennessees, the Eighteenth Regulars and a battery of the Sixth Artillery were sent on an expedition to Ilo Ilo. This was the disposition during the six weeks following the first battles.

Life in the Trenches. Life in the trenches during that period was far from agreeable. It was necessary for the men to keep within the shelter of the breastworks day and night, since sharpshooters from the woods fronting them were constantly pecking away at them, and though at long range, scarcely a day passed without one or more men being hit. Nearly every night the Filipinos opened fire upon the intrenchments after the manner of warfare they had carried on with the Spaniards, which was seldom replied to from our side, although occasional volleys were fired to silence them. All sorts of shelters were constructed by the men to protect themselves from the hot rays of the sun during the middle of the day, most of them consisting of pieces of bamboo matting or strips of galvanized roofing laid upon frames resting upon the crest of the breastworks. Under these shelters the men ate, slept and passed away the time in reading, writing, playing cards, and in any other form of amusement possible under the conditions. They even indulged in ball games a little in the rear of the trenches, but not entirely beyond the range of sharpshooters, becoming careless of their personal safety as time went by. Lieutenant French, of the Montanas, and Captain Elliott and Lieutenant Alford, of the Kansans, were killed in the vicinity of Caloocan.

Preparing for an Attack. The month immediately succeeding the abortive attack upon Manila was one of general anxiety to the foreign population and to the army. It was known that an uprising of the natives was being planned and it was uncertain what proportions it would attain. A population of nearly 300,000, a great majority of whom were of the same race as the insurgents and to a large extent in sympathy with them, offered numbers at least for a serious, if unsuccessful, uprising against the army of occupation. It was simply a matter of ability of the natives to combine in a practical way and their possession of sufficient courage to carry out any general plan agreed upon. It transpired that the Filipinos possessed neither of these important requisites and that there was never, at any time, the real danger which both the authorities and the peaceable inhabitants

15

Part of the Oregon and Minnesota Line in the Street Fight in TonJo, February 23. (See page 19.)

feared. However, scarcely a day passed that the authorities were not warned by men in the employ of the Intelligence Bureau and by self-constituted informants, that certain days, generally Sunday, had been fixed upon for the grand uprising, accompanied by another assault upon the American lines. In accordance with the invariable Filipino custom, this attack and outbreak was to occur in the night time. Many times the troops were kept under arms the entire night, frequently being called out to take their assigned positions in the street, and every night some portion of the troops was held in special readiness for immediate action. Strong guards were maintained on the bridges, at the electric light plant and the penitentiary and other strategic points nightly. So alert were the troops and so well practiced in responding to alarms, that one regiment of the provost guard was roused from a sound sleep and was organized and on the street ready for action within seven minutes from the time the alarm was given. Notwithstanding this vigilance and display of force, a general outbreak was attempted on the night of February 22. On the previous day several hundred armed insurgents made their way through the bayous from Malabon to the Tondo district of the city and kept in hiding until midnight. The plan of operations was for numerous fires to be set in various parts of the city, and then, when the army was fully occupied in subduing these and natural confusion resulted, these armed men were to make a sudden attack, to be joined in by the thousands of sympathizers scattered about the city. It was supposed that this would require the recall of a large number of troops from the lines, which would afford a favorable opportunity for an attack by Aguinaldo's army. This plan failed because of the inability of the insurgents to cooperate on such an extensive scale, and particularly because of the lack of courage necessary on the part of the sympathizers within the city limits.

Early in the evening fires were started in the Santa Cruz district, which were subdued, after much damage had been done, by the joint action of the local fire department, the English fire company and the provost guard. The hose was frequently cut and soldiers were fired upon from roofs and windows of houses, but the action of the troops was so prompt and their marksmanship so good in responding to the fire of the sharpshooters, that no general uprising occurred. Shortly before midnight new fires broke out in the Tondo district at several points, and almost simultaneously Filipino bugles were heard on the streets and an attack was made upon the quarters of the Minnesota troops stationed there. These troops formed under fire and repelled the attack, assisted by a company of the Oregons sent to their relief. Meanwhile the fires had

Great fires of February 22

17

A group of the Twenty-third Regulars after the Capture of the Railroad Iron Barricade in Tondo, February 23.

spread with great rapidity, and rapidly consumed the entire nipa hut district, no effort being made to extinguish it by the Americans, who thought that the natives might be given the privilege of burning their own houses if they desired to do so. A little later still other fires were started near the large market in the San Nicholas District and made rapid progress through the more substantial part of the city, composed almost entirely of the ordinary two story wooden houses, and occupied largely for business purposes by both Chinese and natives. Fearing that this fire would spread to the chief business part of town and to the United States commissary and quartermaster's depots, fire companies were hastily organized among the troops, and everything obtainable in the way of apparatus was utilized, and by the most desperate exertions, lasting from midnight until seven o'clock in the morning, the conflagration was finally checked and subdued. During this time the troops engaged in fighting the fire, as well as the patrols on the streets, were constantly fired upon by skulking sharpshooters, and a bushwhacking warfare was carried on the entire night, resulting in the wounding of several of our own men and the death of a few score of insurgents, the result of our better marksmanship.

Street Fight in Tondo District.

The following morning two companies of the Oregons and two of the Minnesotas formed a line on the edge of Tondo and swept north through the burned district to drive out the remaining insurgents. After they had made considerable progress they were joined by two companies of the Twenty-third Infantry. The fight which followed was a most trying one, the insurgents shooting from behind the many stone walls and fences and the basements of houses, each one of which had to be in turn assaulted and captured by the troops. The severest fighting was around a large garden whose stone walls made a splendid fort, and within which the bodies of many insurgents were found after its capture, also at a strong barricade of railroad iron and stones which the natives had constructed during the night at the Tondo bridge, and which was gallantly charged and captured by our men. The natives were driven into a jungle towards our lines at Caloocan, and managed to effect their escape back to Malabon by the sloughs and bayous by which they had entered the city. More than 100 of them were killed and nearly 200 captured and sent back to the walled city. The loss upon our side was but one man killed and two wounded. Thus ended the great uprising which the natives had counted so much upon, and the anticipation of which had done so much to retard the advance of the army and prevent the commanding general from undertaking an offensive campaign at a distance from the city.

Officers watching the Attack of the Oregons, the Twentieth Regulars and the Sixth Artillery on the City of Pasig.

Wheaton's flying Brigade.

As soon as the first reenforcements were received early in March a special flying brigade was organized under command of General Wheaton, for the purpose of driving the enemy out of the Pasig region and forming a line between Manila and the Laguna de Bahia, thus cutting the Filipino army in two, the ultimate plan being to drive one section of this army to the north and the other section to the south, and prevent an interchange of troops between the two sections. This brigade consisted of the Oregons, Washingtons, the Twentieth Regulars, the Twenty-second Regulars, two troops of the Fourth Cavalry and two guns of the Sixth Artillery. At this time the city of Pasig, lying on an island between the San Mateo river and two branches of the Pasig river, was the base of operations for General Pio del Pilar's army. The first position was at Guadelupe church, fronting San Pedro Macati, standing on a high bluff and protected on its front by an almost impassable ravine. Wheaton's brigade advanced at daylight on the morning of March 13, its right wing swinging around to the left to envelope the flank and rear of the army at Guadelupe.

Capture of Pasig.

After a sharp fight the Filipinos retired to Pasig to prevent being captured, and the Americans occupied the hills bordering the river and overlooking the new Filipino position. The next day the cavalry advanced on the extreme right to Tayguig, which it captured after suffering considerable losses, while the Washingtons made a gallant and successful attack upon Pateros, and one battalion of the Oregons crossed the river and made a flank demonstration upon the Pasig intrenchments fronting the San Mateo river, having a sharp conflict with the concealed enemy across the stream. Other companies of the Oregons took position on the bluffs opposite Pasig and poured volleys into the city, which were returned with spirit by the defenders. The next day Pasig was assaulted by the Twentieth Infantry, which crossed the river under the protection of the fire of the Oregon companies on the bluff and of the battalion of the Oregons which again made a flank attack upon the San Mateo trenches. The advance of the Twentieth was most gallant and determined, and the enemy was driven from street to street and house to house, until the entire city was captured and occupied. Again the following morning a battalion of the Twentieth, sent in pursuit of the retreating Filipinos, encountered them in a strong position at Cainta, from which it drove them after a severe fight. Late that afternoon Pilar's forces made a counter attack upon the Washingtons and two companies of the Oregons that had been stationed at Tayguig, and during the night General Wheaton organized his troops to drive these forces far to the south. At daylight in the morning the Twenty-second, Oregons and Washingtons moved

Noon Bivouac of the Twentieth Regulars on the Hills opposite Pasig.

out to the south in extended order, the left of the Washingtons resting on the Laguna. A running fight was maintained for about ten miles, when pursuit was stopped and the forces returned to their positions of the night before. The Washington regiment was left as a garrison at Pasig and Pateros and the flying brigade returned to Manila, the object of the campaign having been accomplished and the enemy's army cut permanently in two. In holding these positions Captain Fortson and Lieutenant Irwin of the Washingtons were killed.

Filipino Defenses at Malabon. Said the German consul at Manila, when he looked over the ground where the Oregon regiment made its famous charge from the Caloocan trenches and captured the defenses of Malabon, "I take off my hat to the American volunteer." It was indeed a brilliant feat, and one that would have been impossible of accomplishment against an enemy of equal valor, yet there was probably not a regiment in the whole Eighth Army Corps that would not have charged over the same ground and performed the same work had it been ordered to do so. They were all disciplined soldiers who had been tried in the fire of battle and proved genuine gold.

For seven weeks the two armies lay behind breastworks, the American line extending from the Malabon pike around Caloocan southeastward past La Loma church and on towards the water-works, while the Filipino line was between the Americans and the Tuliahan river. The insurrectos improved this period of inaction on our part by constructing a most elaborate system of intrenchments, in some places there being four lines of works, one behind the other, covering a distance of half a mile from first to last. The impregnable nature of some of them is shown by the engraving opposite. Perfectly sheltered by them, the insurgents fired upon our men by thrusting their guns through the little port holes, only in the end to abandon the works and flee in terror as our steadily advancing lines arrived so close that they feared a hand-to-hand conflict. They could not understand the unflinching courage of troops that could advance across the open under fire from such defenses and not falter, and fled rather than encounter them at close range. No wonder the German consul doffed his cap. The American volunteer well earned the tribute that day, no matter to what regiment he belonged or in what part of the field he shed lustre upon his country's honor.

Battle of Malabon. March 25 was the day selected by General Otis for the forward movement upon Malolos, to be inaugurated by an assault upon the enemy's intrenched line, the plan of battle being to swing our right flank around to the left and coop up the enemy in Malabon and force a surrender. Four brigades were used, commanded by Wheaton, Hale, Hall and H. G. Otis, McArthur being the division commander. After dark on the

One of the Trenches Defending Malabon, Stormed by the Second Oregon Volunteers, March 25, 1899.

24th, the Kansas regiment was moved out of the intrenchments it had constructed and occupied so long on the extreme left, and which were fronted by the heaviest Filipino defenses, the Oregon regiment taking its position. The Kansas were placed in the line farther to the right.

Colorados and Minnesotas at Maraquina.

The movement began on the extreme right at daylight by the Minnesotas and Colorados, of General Hall's brigade, advancing and cutting off the insurgents that made their headquarters at Maraquina, on the San Mateo river above Santolan, from the army defending Malabon. This was not done without severe fighting, in which Captain Stewart of the Colorados was killed, but the object of cutting the enemy's force in two was gained. A counter attack was made the following night by the insurrectos on two companies of the Colorados, but they kept the enemy at bay until support from the Minnesotas arrived, when the natives fled. Almost simultaneously with this cutting movement the right wing of the force attacking Malabon was set in motion. This was General Hale's brigade, composed of the Nebraskas, South Dakotas and Pennsylvanias, followed, but a few minutes later, by General H. G. Otis' brigade, consisting of the Montanas, Kansans and Third Artillery as infantry. With these brigades were two guns of the Utah Artillery, two guns of the Sixth Artillery and a Colt's automatic machine gun. The plan of the movement was for these two brigades to swing around to the left, the right of Wheaton's brigade at Caloocan being the pivotal point, and endeavor to inclose the enemy's army in Malabon and capture it. Wheaton's brigade consisted of the Oregons on the extreme left, facing the almost impregnable defenses of Malabon, the Twenty-second Regulars, two guns of the Utah Artillery and one Hotchkiss revolving cannon in the line, with the Third Regulars in support. Complete success of this plan would have rendered an assault upon the Malabon defenses unnecessary, as the insurrectos would have been flanked out of them, but the assault was made and the American volunteer again earned undying fame.

Advance of Otis and Hale.

As Otis' and Hale's brigades advanced they encountered strong opposition. They were compelled to cross long open spaces under a terrific fire from intrenchments concealed in the bamboo forests fringing the Malabon river. At intervals the lines halted and poured volleys into the woods in their front, and then rose and advanced again. The insurgents were driven from the first line of intrenchments in this way, and fell back to a second, but were in turn swept from this by the resistless advance of the American troops. In this way, in some places four, and in others three, lines of intrenchments were successively carried before

Rear of one of the Filipino Trenches Captured in the Attack on the Malabon Defenses, March 25.

the Tuliahan river was reached, the extreme right covering about ten miles in its grand sweep to that point. At the river the resistance was stronger than ever and the fighting more desperate. Hale's brigade crossed the river and bivouacked for the night on the opposite side. A portion of Otis' brigade also crossed the river, the resistance being especially severe in front of the Kansas and Third Artillery lines, and the losses of those organizations being heavy. The latter was the first to cross the stream and drive the Filipinos from their strong defenses on the other side. They held their positions during the night and advanced again the following day.

Impatient at the time consumed in making this turning movement in the face of desperate resistance, General Wheaton ordered an advance of his brigade against the Malabon intrenchments, and then it was that the Oregons leaped over their breastworks and rushed upon the Filipino trenches, the nearest of which were but one hundred yards distant from the extreme left of the line and approachable only through a slough in which the advancing men sank to the hips at every step. Farther to the right the first line was more distant, but the ground was open and had to be crossed under a terrific fire. The fire of musketry and the yells of triumph were incessant for an hour as the volunteers swept over trench after trench and drove the enemy without pause, until all had sought safety behind the defenses on the opposite side of the river or within the heavily fortified lines of Malabon, fronted by almost impassable bayous. The only means of crossing the river here was a stone bridge at the village of Tenajeros and the railroad bridge just above, both of which had been partially destroyed by the enemy. The line was halted near the river, and during the remainder of the day it fought the enemy posted behind the trenches defending these bridges, having only such shelter as could be hastily improvised, and subjected to a severe cross fire on the left from masses of insurrectos in the unapproachable defenses in the edge of Malabon, in an effort to subdue this flank fire, that assault upon a partially destroyed bridge leading into Malabon, one platoon alone losing three killed and six wounded. The Twenty-second Regulars advanced on the right of the Oregons and shared with them the labor and glory of the attack, while a portion of the Third Regulars came up in support and had its share of the fighting. Four troops of the Fourth Cavalry were sent into the fight at various places in the line and did the same splendid work as all their comrades.

Wheaton's Assault at Malabon.

Work of the South Dakotas at Maycauayan, March 27.

Had a further advance been ordered, the Filipinos could have been driven from their intrenched positions across the river in front of Wheaton's brigade, and the troops could have crossed the stream and covered the road leading out of Malabon that afternoon, but the original plan of having the extreme right swing around was adhered to and the left was held back, with the result that the Filipinos set fire to Malabon early the following morning and evacuated the town along the road that might have been closed to them the night before. Thus a great battle had been won, impregnable intrenchments stormed and captured, and lasting glory shed upon American arms, but the enemy was allowed to escape and the best fruits of the victory were lost.

The next morning the advance of Wheaton's brigade, which should have been made the evening before, was commenced. The Filipinos were driven by the Oregons from their intrenchments defending the Tenajeros bridge, and the regiment crossed to the other side. The bridge was sufficiently rebuilt for the passage of the artillery and the wagon train, and then the forward movement was taken up. During the entire forenoon a stream of refugees and soldiers poured northward from Malabon along the road within easy shelling distance from the artillery posted near the bridge, but because of the large number of women and children among them they were not fired upon, and in this way the entire Filipino army escaped. About noon the advance began, the Oregons on the extreme left moving toward Polo, and the Third and Twenty-second Regulars upon the right advancing upon Malinta. Several successive lines of breastworks were captured during the advance, the fighting along the railroad approaching Malinta being especially severe. It was here that General Egbert and Lieutenant Krayenbuhl, of the regulars, were killed. About the middle of the afternoon the Oregons, having advanced on the left almost to Polo, were withdrawn to Malinta, which had just been captured by the right wing of the brigade. This was the end of the work of Wheaton's brigade, which had only been loaned to General McArthur from Anderson's division for the capture of Malabon. The advance from this point upon Malolos was made by the brigades of Hale and H. G. Otis, which pushed on that afternoon beyond Malinta as far as Polo. The next day the advance was resumed and some of the most severe fighting of the campaign was had in the vicinity of Maycauayan and the Marilao river. It was here that the only genuine effort at a counter attack was made by the Filipinos, Aguinaldo's red legged regiment being brought forward from Malolos by train for this purpose. This

Advance on Malolos.

A Game of Cards in the Trenches. (See page 15.)

was the best body of troops in the Filipino army, and was composed of men who had seen service in the Spanish army before the capture of Manila. They were fairly well drilled and disciplined and when they deployed in the open field beyond Marilao for the attack they presented a very business-like appearance, but it was only a short time after the attack began before they realized their mistake. The South Dakotas, Montanas and the Third Artillery made short work of them, and those who did not seek safety in flight were buried on the ground. Lieutenants Adams, Morrison and Lien, of the South Dakotas, were killed here and Lieutenant Gregg, of the regulars, at Malolos. A great deal had been said about the defenses of Malolos, and it was expected that the assault would be a desperate one, but after the troops had carried the defenses at the Bocaue river and the intrenchments near Bigaa, there was little opposition to the entrance to the city, which the American troops entered and occupied on the twenty-ninth of March, the Filipinos having retired to a strong position at Calumpit, beyond the Bag Bag river. McArthur's army then rested from its labors, strong detachments being placed at all strategic points between Manila and Malolos and the railroad put in good operating condition for the supply of the army at the front.

During the period of inactivity early in April, the Filipinos maintained a base of operations at Santa Maria, a small town in the foothills four miles east of Bocaue. Several scouting parties sent out by the two companies of the Minnesotas at Bocaue and three companies of the Oregons at Marilao, demonstrated the fact that the Filipinos were in strong force at Santa Maria, but no effort was made to dislodge them. Encouraged by this immunity from attack, they planned a raid upon Bocaue and Marilao for the purpose of destroying the railroad bridges at those places. About midnight, April 10, some 500 of them suddenly attacked the two Minnesota companies, which were on opposite sides of the Bocaue river and not within good supporting distance of each other. The companies bravely defended themselves until morning, one of them being compelled to abandon its camp and take up a new position in the dark, while the other, in an endeavor to cross the river to relieve the other company, was challenged in English by the Filipino commander and was fired upon when the commander responded to the challenge by giving the name of the organization. Relief was sent from Bigaa, a little further up the track, where another detachment of the Minnesotas was stationed, and with it came an armored car in which was mounted a machine gun. There being no locomotive at that point the car was shoved down the track by soldiers. A body of the enemy made a rush upon it,

Night Attack on Minnesotas.

The Tenth Pennsylvanias Building Trenches at the Extreme Front.

apparently not realizing its nature, but when the machine gun opened upon them they scattered and fled, leaving a number of dead upon the ground to pay for their rashness. At daylight the Minnesotas advanced upon their assailants and drove them back to Santa Maria with considerable losses.

Night Attack on Oregons. The attack upon the Oregons at Marilao the same night was carefully planned. The camp was surrounded on three sides, Filipino lines extending across the railroad track both above and below the camp. The telegraph wires were cut so that aid could not be sent for, and when everything was ready signal rockets were fired from both sides to give notice that the attack was to begin. It was about three o'clock in the morning when the assailants opened up with volleys, firing into the tents where the men were sleeping, at a distance of about 400 yards. The men scrambled out of their tents and were lined up by their officers in the rice fields on both sides of the track, and with only the rice paddies for protection, responded to the attack, the return fire from the Americans beginning within a minute from the time the first shot was fired by the Filipinos. The combat lasted until daylight, when the enemy withdrew without having made any further advance than the point from which the first volley was fired. Both of these attacks, well planned as they were, and made by a sufficient force to have been successful, failed because the Filipinos did not have the necessary courage to push home their assault and make a determined rush upon the Americans. Their only hope of success lay in the surprise, and when they wasted the first precious moments of the attack in firing from a distance, they let slip the golden opportunity, for it was hopeless to charge the Americans after they had once organized for defense. An Oregon outpost was cut off and three men were killed and one severely wounded.

Burning of Santa Maria. The day following this night attack, two battalions of the Oregons and two battalions of the Minnesotas, with one three inch gun and one Hotchkiss revolving cannon, were concentrated at Bocaue, under the command of General Wheaton, for the purpose of driving the Filipinos from their stronghold at Santa Maria. At daybreak on the morning of April 12, line was formed and the movement up the Bocaue river was begun. The enemy was encountered about a mile from Santa Maria, but was easily driven back and soon abandoned the town, retreating north to Angat. It was learned afterwards from two Spanish refugees who had been prisoners in the Filipinos' hands, as well as from Chinese residents of Santa Maria, that Aguinaldo himself was in the town at the time of this attack, and that he had come there several days

Landing Stores from Cascoes on the Laguna de Bahia.

previously to superintend the attack which had been made upon Bocaue and Marilao; and further, that the enemy had been celebrating what they were pleased to consider a great victory over the Americans on that occasion. Aguinaldo hastily fled on horseback less than half an hour before the American troops entered the town. Had his presence been known, it is probable a little more energy on our part would have resulted in his capture. Santa Maria was burned and the entire surrounding country laid waste as a military measure to prevent its being used as a base of operations for flank attacks upon the railroad line, and then the troops returned to their former stations, leaving a trail of smoke behind them that could be seen for miles. This was one of the severest blows struck at the enemy during the campaign, and did more to convince the insurrectos that the Americans were in earnest than any other single event of the war. Positive orders against burning houses were then issued and enforced.

Capture of Santa Cruz. The next movement made by General Otis was the dispatch of an expedition under General Lawton across the Laguna de Bahia for the capture of the town of Santa Cruz, the chief port on the southeastern shore of the lake. This movement consisted of about 1,800 men drawn from the North Dakotas, Idahos, Fourteenth Infantry and Sixth Artillery. They were embarked on cascoes, which were towed by gunboats. Their appearance was a great surprise to the insurgents and to the people of Santa Cruz, who were astonished to learn that the Americans were not cooped up in Manila, as they had been told was the case by the leaders of the insurrection. They did not recover from their astonishment until the Americans had landed, deployed their lines before the city and advanced upon it, when they fled in disorder, the portion of the insurgents who made resistance leaving many of their dead behind them. This was the first knowledge the inhabitants of that section of the island had of the successes of the Americans. Systematic deception by the leaders of the insurrection as to the course of events had led these people, as well as the inhabitants of all sections where our troops had not yet made their appearance, to believe that the Filipino arms had been triumphant everywhere, and that the Americans were closely besieged in Manila and would soon be overwhelmed and driven into the bay. After occupying Santa Cruz two or three days the American troops withdrew, leaving the town again to the occupation of the insurrectos, thus rendering the expedition of no practical value, unless it be that some advantage was gained by undeceiving the people of that region as to the universal success of the insurrectos.

1—Soldiers in Cascoes for an Expedition on the Laguna. 2—Bull Train at Bocaue ready for the Advance of Lawton's Troops on Norzagaray. 3—Filipino Boiler Iron Defenses at Cañumpit Captured by the Kansans, Nebraskas, South Dakotas, Iowas, Third Artillery and Utah Battery. 4—Twenty-second Regulars in the Jungle in the Advance of Wheaton's Flying Brigade on Pasig

Advance to the North.

After the capture of Malolos, the Filipino government established a new capital at San Isidro, in Nueva Ecija province, on the Rio Grande de Pampanga, some 30 miles farther to the north and about 10 miles east of the railroad. The new plan of campaign decided upon was for McArthur's division to push north along the railroad, while Lawton with a provisional division should move northward parallel with the railroad and distant about 15 miles from it, clearing the country between the railroad and the mountains and driving the enemy north to his northern base or eastward into the mountains, whither the insurgents had been accustomed to retreat when pursued to this point by the Spaniards in previous insurrections.

Byac ne Bato.

Only a few miles from San Miguel, an important town on Lawton's road, lies a Filipino mountain stronghold, Byac ne Bato, a place the Spaniards have never been able to capture. It was to this stronghold the Filipinos retreated in the insurrection of 1897, and it was here that the Spaniards suffered severe losses in their efforts to capture the place. It is a small valley nestling in the mountains and only approached by a mountain trail easily defended by a few men. It receives its name from one of the peaks near it, which has a split top, the name indicating, in the Tagalog language, a cleft mountain. Unable to capture this place, the Spaniards finally ended the rebellion by paying Aguinaldo and his immediate friends 400,000 Mexican dollars, upon the receipt of which these leaders abandoned the contest and expatriated themselves to Hong Kong and Singapore. This money was deposited in a bank at Hong Kong and is still a subject of litigation among the various Filipino claimants.

Capture of Norzagaray.

Lawton's advance consisted of a provisional brigade under Colonel Summers of the Oregon regiment, composed of the Oregons and Minnesotas, with two guns of the Sixth Artillery and one troop of the Fourth Cavalry. This brigade moved out from Bocaue on the twenty-third of April and advanced through Santa Maria to Norzagaray, on the Quingua river, encountering the enemy on the outskirts of town late in the afternoon. After driving the Filipinos into the town, the brigade encamped until morning, when it resumed the advance, and drove the enemy from the town. A column was sent the same morning down the river and captured the town of Angat, which had until recently been the headquarters of the army of General Gregorio del Pilar operating in that vicinity, and where a large hospital for the Filipino wounded had been maintained. The command rested for two days at Norzagaray, awaiting the arrival of General Lawton, who had started north from La Loma by the way of Novaliches, with the North Dakotas, the Third and

The North Dakotas Halting for a Rest in the Advance from Angat to Bustos, near the Quingua River.

Twenty-second Infantry, four guns of the Sixth Artillery and a troop of the Fourth Cavalry. While awaiting the arrival of General Lawton on the second day of occupation of Norzagaray, Colonel Summers' forces were attacked from across the stream by a body of the enemy who had stolen up under cover of the forest and suddenly opened fire upon men who were swimming in the river. There were at the time fully 100 men in the water, as well as a large number of cavalry horses and water buffalo, and strange to say not one of these was hit by the hundreds of bullets that struck all around them. There was a lively scrambling for places of safety, and in a few minutes the fire of the insurgents was returned and in about an hour they were driven away.

Capture of Baliuag. Upon the arrival of General Lawton the command moved down the river to Angat and Moranco. The next day Colonel Summers' command proceeded to San Rafael, from which the enemy retired without firing a shot, but the troops were recalled the same day upon telegraphic orders from General Otis, because of the opening of peace negotiations by General Luna, whose army had been severely worsted in battle the day before by McArthur's division at Calumpit. In a few days these negotiations fell through and Lawton's advance was resumed. On the first of May San Rafael was again occupied by Summers' brigade, but this time a hard fight was necessary for its capture. At the same time Lawton's troops passed down the opposite side of the river and had a sharp conflict with the enemy. The next day an advance was made from San Rafael to Baliuag, the Third Infantry being in the lead. After a conflict in which our troops suffered a few losses and the enemy lost quite heavily, the town was entered and occupied shortly after noon, and was made the headquarters for General Lawton for his operations in that vicinity. Baliuag was garrisoned at that time and the garrison has ever since been maintained there by the Third Infantry. Two days later the brigade of Colonel Summers was again pushed to the front as far as the town of Maasin, seven miles farther to the north, where the enemy's intrenchments were stormed and captured by the Minnesotas after a brief resistance.

San Ildefonso and San Miguel. The Filipinos retreated to the town of San Ildefonso, where they took up a very strong position, which was really the defense of San Miguel and the road leading to Byac ne Bato. The division rested in this position for the entire week by direction of General Otis, because of information he had received that General Pio del Pilar was making a raid on Lawton's flank and rear with 5,000 men, which information was

1—Fourteenth Regulars in Captured Filipino Trenches at Pasay. 2—Minnesotas in Line near Baliuag Waiting Orders to Advance. 3—Ward for Filipino Wounded in the American Hospital at Manila. 4—Tossing in a Blanket, a Favorite Amusement when the Soldiers have a "Rough House."

proved, by a week's scouting and loss of time, to be untrue, and the advance was resumed. A small body of scouts, under the leadership of W. H. Young, a civilian, made a demonstration against San Ildefonso at daylight in the morning, and, by working backwards and forwards along the Filipino front, so demoralized the enemy's forces of 1,500 men that they abandoned the town and retired to San Miguel. The scouts, supported by one company of the Oregons and one of the Minnesotas, followed the insurgents and drove them out of San Miguel in the same way in which they had driven them from San Ildefonso, and that night the army occupied both of those places. Unfortunately, Chief Scout Young was mortally wounded, dying the next day at the hospital in Manila, to which he was hastily conveyed.

Capture of San Isidro.

From San Miguel General Lawton sent a battalion of the Third Infantry to make a demonstration towards Byac ne Bato, but no enemy was discovered defending the approach thereto, and as information from various persons was to the effect that but a small body of the enemy had entered the stronghold, it was decided to pay no attention to that place, but to push on to the north to the Filipino capital. Accordingly, Summers' brigade was again sent out on the forward movement, and after several encounters with the enemy, who were defeated and driven backward in every combat, the brigade arrived before San Isidro on the afternoon of the sixteenth of May. It was here that the scouts made their famous charge across Turbon bridge, described elsewhere in this volume. It was expected that the defense of San Isidro would be strong, and next morning the Twenty-second Infantry and one battalion of the North Dakotas were brought to the front and deployed with the first battalion of the Oregons, four guns of the artillery being brought up to support the movement. When the advance was made it was discovered that the only resistance was in front of the Oregons and North Dakotas, where a sharp fight was maintained for half an hour, resulting in the rout of the enemy and capture of the town.

After remaining several days in San Isidro, the town was evacuated, the Third Infantry returning by way of San Rafael to Baliuag and the remainder of Lawton's command going south along the Rio Grande de Pampanga to a new base of operations established at Candaba a few days previously by the Seventeenth Infantry and the river gunboats. On this march the Oregons had a sharp conflict with the enemy at San Antonio, having crossed the stream for the purpose of driving the Filipinos back towards their new base of operations at Tarlac, on the railroad. The Third Infantry also had a running fight from San Ildefonso to

41

Burial Party of the Iowas after the Advance on Calumpit.

Baliuag, being attacked by the forces of the enemy which had taken refuge at Byac ne Bato. This fight was quite severe, and the enemy were driven at every point where they were encountered. The Filipinos reoccupied the town when our forces abandoned it, and it again became the seat of government. They celebrated their reoccupation by murdering a number of Chinamen and natives who were suspected of having been friendly to the Americans.

One of the objects of this northern trip was to gain possession of the large number of Spanish prisoners and the few Americans in the possession of the Filipino army, but this was not accomplished, as the Filipinos removed their prisoners to a point farther into the interior several days before the city was captured. In one of the rooms of a large prison building in which the Spaniards and Americans had been confined at San Isidro, was discovered a portion of a diary kept by one of the American prisoners, and on the wall was a complete roster of the Americans then in the hands of the Filipinos, numbering only fourteen persons, including Lieutenant Gilmore and seven seamen from the gunboat Yorktown, who had been captured some time before while making a reconnoissance on the coast. The Spanish prisoners number about 2,000, most of whom were captured before the fall of Manila by being cut off while doing garrison duty in towns remote from the city. Spain had offered Aguinaldo $7,000,000 for their release, but the United States would not permit the transaction to be carried out. These unfortunate men are still in the hands of the Filipinos, though there is no war between their captors and Spain, but they are Aguinaldo's trump card, and he will not give them up without something good in return.

Prisoners held by Filipinos.

Simultaneously with Lawton's advance in the interior McArthur moved his division against the heavily intrenched positions of General Luna's army at the Bag Bag river and Calumpit. This movement was participated in by the Kansans, Iowas, Montanas, South Dakotas, Nebraskas, Third Artillery, Sixth Artillery and Utah Battery and some of the most severe fighting of the war resulted. The Filipinos had constructed most elaborate intrenchments, many of them proof against the heaviest field artillery we possessed, and these intrenchments had to be stormed by the infantry. It was in this advance that Colonel Stotsenberg, of the Nebraskas, was killed. The lines advanced from trench to trench and river to river, driving the enemy before them, crossing open fields under terrific fire, and even fording the Bag Bag river, waist deep, under the fire of the enemy. The defense of the Filipinos was stubborn, but at no time were they able to stop the

The Bag Bag and Calumpit.

The Work of One Shell from the Utah Battery in the Battle of Caloocan, February 10. (See Page 13.)

advancing lines, and they always abandoned their trenches in time to save themselves from the slaughter they knew to be certain to be their lot if they undertook to hold them until the Americans had actually reached them. It was in leading the Kansas regiment across the river to flank the heavy trenches at Calumpit that Colonel Funston won his brigadier's star. The losses of the Filipinos were extremely heavy, and it was at this time that General Luna sent a commissioner through the lines ostensibly to interview General Otis on terms of peace. Because of this act on his part offensive operations were discontinued, but it transpired, as the negotiations advanced, that General Luna was only negotiating for a suspension of hostilities, and that, in fact, he was only making a play to gain a few days' time until he got his army into a strong position at San Fernando, a few miles farther up the road. When this fact was developed hostilities were again resumed. While General Lawton was at San Isidro, General McArthur's command advanced to Santo Tomas, and a little later again advanced to San Fernando, which he captured after a brief struggle, and which became a new base of operations for his division, and so remains to the present time.

During the time the campaign on the north was in progress, the entire south and east lines were inactive. The sound of insurgent rifles was heard almost nightly by the people in Manila, as the insurrectos made their usual bushwhacking attacks upon our outposts. The Washingtons holding the Pasig region had frequent conflicts with bands of the enemy, while the Colorados at the Santolan pumping station were constantly annoyed by them. It was determined to sweep them out of the Pasig region and Maraquina and then to drive them from their strong positions on the south. These movements were made under the direct command of General Lawton, though General Otis maintained supervision over the whole. The first movement was made in the Pasig region, with the intention of cooping up the enemy in the town of Taytay, at the head of the west branch of the Laguna de Bahia, and capturing the forces there if possible. For this purpose General Hall was sent across the Maraquina valley to get in the rear of Taytay, while General Lawton himself, with the Washingtons, North Dakotas, Twelfth Infantry and Sixth Artillery made an assault upon the town from the south and west. General Hall's forces consisted of the Oregons, Colorados and a portion of the Fourth Regulars and a troop of the Fourth Cavalry with Hawthorne's Battery of mountain guns. This brigade left the pumping station before daylight on the third of June and moved across the Maraquina valley into the mountains that rise almost abruptly from it on the east. Here the

The Morong Campaign.

45

Troops Wading Out to Embark on Cascoes on the Laguna.

enemy were encountered in strong positions in the hills, from which they were driven by the Oregons. The column then followed the fleeing enemy south towards Taytay and Antipolo over a very rough mountain road. Within about a mile of the road leading from Taytay to Antipolo, which was the line of retreat from Taytay that General Hall's advance was intended to close, the Filipinos were again encountered in an extremely strong position on three hills commanding a flat, over which the troops were compelled to advance. They poured in a hot fire upon the cavalry as it deployed upon the flat and checked its advance. The Oregons were then ordered up, and rapidly deploying one battalion against each hill, they charged up the steep sides and drove the enemy from all three positions. Meanwhile the sounds of conflict at Taytay, some two miles distant, were very plainly heard, but General Hall failed to push on to the Antipolo road, encamping for the night on the scene of his last conflict, and thus the road was left open for the retreat of the army driven out by the gallant work of the Washingtons, North Dakotas and Twelfth Infantry. The next morning the Colorados advanced to Antipolo with but little opposition, while the Washingtons and Dakotas were put on cascoes and were towed by gunboats to the eastern arm of the Laguna, for the purpose of capturing the town of Morong. They arrived opposite the town in the afternoon, and were compelled to wade ashore in the shallow water a distance of several hundred yards, but were not fired upon by the Filipinos until after they had landed and begun their advance on the town. The insurgents opened with a volley from their trenches on the edge of the town, which were immediately swept by volleys from the advancing line. Then the troops charged with the same fierce yells that had so many times struck terror to the Filipino heart, and the enemy fled without taking chances with the Americans at close quarters. The next day Hall's brigade advancing from Antipolo reached Morong, and the campaign was over, the Filipinos having taken refuge in the mountains to the north. A garrison was left to occupy Morong permanently, and the remainder of the troops returned to their former positions in and around the city.

Paranaque, Las Pinas and Bakur.

Immediately following the Morong campaign, General Lawton turned his attention to clearing Cavite province of the insurrectos whose presence so near the city had been a constant reminder to the people that the rebel army was still active and aggressive. The American lines had not been advanced in that direction since the morning after the attack upon the city. During all this period of four months the insurrectos had intrenched themselves strongly at Paranaque, Las Pinas and Bakur. It was here that the most desperate

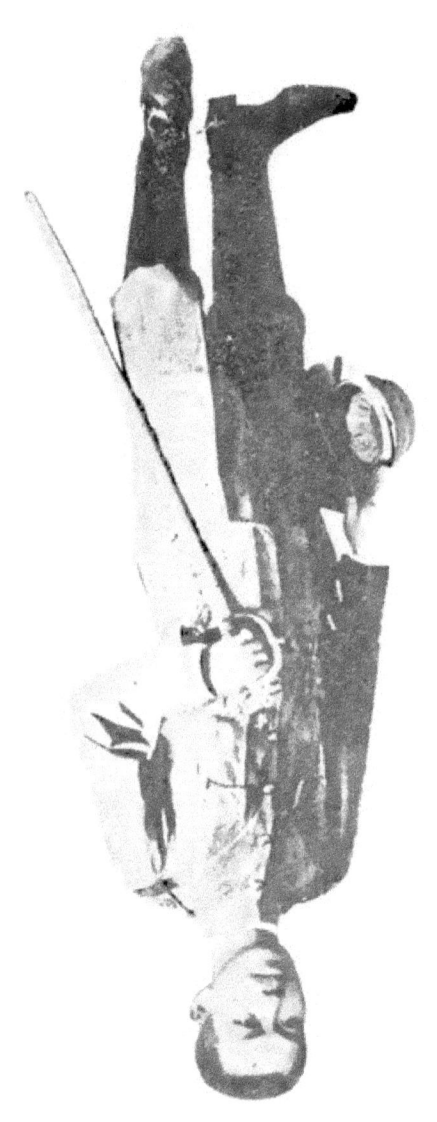

Emilio Aguinaldo y Fame, President of La Republika Filipina.

conflicts between the Spaniards and Filipinos had occurred in previous revolutions, the topography of that swampy country being such as to render offensive operations extremely difficult, and to offer a good natural defense for a small body of men against a much larger attacking force. The troops employed by General Lawton were the Colorados, the Idahos, the Fourteenth, Thirteenth and Twelfth Regulars, and portions of the Fourth Cavalry, the Sixth Artillery and Hawthorne's battery. Vessels of the fleet assisted somewhat in shelling positions within their range, but the shallowness of the water prevented them from coming in close enough to do effective service south of Paranaque. Lawton swung his line far around to the south and west with the intention of inclosing the enemy if possible, but like all other efforts of this kind, the movement failed of its object, and the Filipinos, after a desperate resistance, retired to the southward before their line of retreat could be closed. The fight at Paranaque was extremely severe and our losses were very heavy, though far less than the losses inflicted upon the enemy. Having captured the strong intrenchments about Paranaque, the army advanced against an almost equally strong position at Las Pinas, a few miles farther to the south, and after capturing this, again advanced on still other defenses at Bakur. These were also captured in the same brilliant and gallant manner which had characterized the assaults upon the previous defenses. The retreating army was pursued until it scattered in various directions, and the American troops advanced as far south as Imus, which is still held as an advanced position, garrisons being left at every important point. The fighting was almost continuous in this movement for five days, and the results obtained were the driving of the insurgents from all their strong positions in Cavite province, and the breaking up of their organization in the region which had been the leading insurrectionary district in all rebellions.

Aguinaldo's Government. Aguinaldo's first headquarters, when he was organizing his forces, after the battle of Manila bay, were at Cavite. Soon after General Anderson arrived with the first expedition in July, the headquarters were removed to Bakur, where a provisional revolutionary government was organized. After the fall of Manila the Filipino headquarters were removed to Antipolo and a little later to Malolos, in Bulucan province, on the railroad about thirty miles north of Manila. Here a congress was assembled for the purpose of framing a constitution for the proposed government. This congress was not an elective one, but was composed of men selected by the leaders of the revolution who were residents of only five of the twenty-eight provinces of Luzon island. The men composing the congress were of the limited educated class constituting the aristocracy

49

The Filipino Congress in Session at Malolos Adopting the Constitution for La Republica Filipina.

of the island. This governing class, which is at the head of the revolution, consists almost entirely of people of mixed blood, the Chinese mixture predominating, though there is considerable of the Spanish strain among them. They are generally known as Chinese Mestizos, and most of them are wealthy, are fairly well educated, dress well, live in luxury, and are extremely courteous and hospitable.

Filipino Congress. The sessions of this congress were held in the hall of the fine government building at Malolos, and were almost continuous for several months. The constitution was completed and adopted by the body framing it without submission to the people, and was proclaimed about the middle of January, and Aguinaldo, who had been elected president by the congress, as provided for in its constitution, was installed as president of the new Republica Filipinas. Thus the constitution was framed and adopted and the government organized and established by the sole act of a small group of the Mestizo class, and the people at large were given no voice in the matter whatever. The provisions of the constitution were such as to enable this small class to remain permanently in power, and the government was, in fact, not a democratic one, but that of a small oligarchy possessing complete control over the lives and fortunes of the multitude. This self-constituted congress continued in session after the new constitution had been proclaimed until it was scattered by the Americans advancing upon the Malolos seat of government.

Peace Commissioners. A new capital was then established at San Isidro, thirty miles further to the north and ten miles east of the railroad, where the congress met again by a proclamation of the president on the fifth of May to consider the question of negotiating for terms of peace. In the account of McArthur's advance upon Calumpit it has been related how General Luna sought to gain time by sending an ostensible peace commission to Manila. Luna had at this time, as secretary of war, made himself commander-in-chief of the army, and was opposed to any peace agreement that was not compatible with his personal interests. When the Filipino congress convened at San Isidro in May, it was voted to send a committee of seven to Manila to confer with General Otis and the American commissioners upon the subject of the termination of hostilities and the organization of a government along the lines of a proclamation which had been issued by the American commissioners. This was not satisfactory to General Luna, who expressed his disapprobation in genuine Filipino style. He withdrew all forces except those commanded by officers in close sympathy with him, and then made an effort to capture the peace committee. Three of these he secured and beheaded,

General Gregorio del Pilar and other Peace Commissioners at San Isidro sent to General Lawton by General Luna.

A Company of Insurgent Troops near Parañaque.

General Garcia and the Filipino Garrison at Calbuican before the Town was Captured.

two of them escaped to Manila, and two others combined their interests with his. This was the condition of affairs when General Lawton captured San Isidro. General Gregorio del Pilar, in command of the forces operating in that vicinity and acting as the representative of General Lawton, sent word to General Lawton that a peace commission desired to go to Manila, and General Lawton sent Major J. F. Case, engineer officer, and Major Penrose, surgeon, both of his staff, some distance from the lines to meet General Pilar and other members of the commission, who were brought into San Isidro, and forwarded to Manila by the way of San Rafael and Baliuag. When these men reached Manila it transpired that they were not there for the purpose of arranging terms of peace, but were only playing the same game that Luna had played at Calumpit, requesting only a suspension of hostilities for a period of time, with no definite purpose to be accomplished, except to delay offensive operations on our part until the rainy season had set in, during which season active campaigning is almost impossible. The alleged peace commissioners went back to their chief without having accomplished anything, and this was the end of what was supposed, in the United States, to be a genuine effort on the part of the Filipinos to terminate hostilities. A few weeks later, Luna himself was assassinated by the Aguinaldo faction.

filipino Army.
The army organized by Aguinaldo and his fellow leaders of the insurrection is a nondescript affair, composed chiefly of boys and young men from 15 to 25 years of age, and of every degree of military training, from the regularly enrolled and disciplined soldier down to the undisciplined bushwhacker. Its enrolled force was supposed to number about 70,000 men at the time of the outbreak of the rebellion, of whom about 40,000 were armed with Mausers and Remingtons and the remainder with bolos. The plan of organization was to combine riflemen and bolomen in one regiment, the bolomen being used to supply ammunition and to carry the dead and wounded from the field and to take the place of all disabled riflemen. In this way all of the guns were kept in action, no matter how many casualties the regiment suffered, and no guns were withdrawn from the fight in order that the dead and wounded might be cared for. It was a mystery at first how the enemy carried their dead and wounded from the field, and why it was that scarcely a gun was captured, even when scores of the dead and wounded fell into our hands. The work of the bolomen explains all this. Of course it was originally supposed, and freely boasted of by the Filipinos before hostilities began, that these bolomen were going to do something more warlike than to carry off the dead and wounded.

General Gregorio del Pilar and a Battalion of the Troops that Contested Lawton's Advance on San Isidro.

They expected to charge the Americans and slaughter them with bolos, but after the first morning's light, when the Americans did the charging and slaughtering themselves, this idea of carving the "Americans" with bolos was abandoned. The usual stretcher for carrying off the Filipino dead and wounded was a sort of half-basket woven of bamboo, such as is shown in the foreground of one of the trench scenes on page 74.

Disciplined Filipino Troops. The best disciplined troops in Aguinaldo's army were those which had seen service in the Spanish army, and these amounted to about 5,000 in number. They were under very fair discipline and drill, and when in action fired very good volleys. Their officers watched the Americans very closely during the period before the outbreak, and adopted some of our tactics and many of our words of command. It seemed very strange, and was sometimes extremely deceptive during a combat in the dark, to hear commands given in English by the Filipino officers. Such commands were frequently heard, often accompanied by words not in the drill regulations, but too often heard in the army. The bulk of the Filipino army was organized on the territorial plan; that is, each locality raised its own troops for operations in its own vicinity. The drilled and disciplined troops constituted a sort of regular army, but a majority of the insurrectionary forces were of this militia class, and this fact accounts very largely for the inability of the Filipinos to mass a large force at any point for offensive operations, since the bulk of the troops were only available for service in the vicinity of their towns.

Filipino Uniform and Flag. The uniform of the regular Filipino troops consists of a light striped blue drilling, very serviceable for wear in the tropics and almost identical with that worn by the Spanish army. The majority of the uniformed soldiers wore shoes, but the great bulk of the army went barefooted. Accustomed to going barefooted from childhood, the Filipino's feet are as tough as leather, and he can tramp over rough places and bamboo thorns with impunity. He is thus better equipped for campaigning through the sloughs and rice fields than the American soldier, who is compelled to wear shoes. Most of the soldiers wear a broad-brimmed straw hat, turned up in the front and drooping down in the back to shade the back of the neck. The regular troops fasten the portion turned up with a little rosette of red and blue, the Filipino colors, in the center of which is fastened a triangle, with the sun engraved in the middle and one star in each of the corners. The Filipino flag consists of two longitudinal stripes of red and blue with a triangular wedge of white at the end, on which are embroidered or painted a sun in the center and a star in each corner in silver or gold. This triangular

An Insurgent Battalion in the Outskirts of Manila after its Capture by the Americans.

device with the sun and stars is the symbol of the Katipunans, a secret revolutionary order, which is the backbone of the insurrection. These Katipunans terrorize the rest of the population and compel them to participate in the insurrection under the penalty of having their throats cut. Through the fear of such summary vengeance on the part of the Katipunans, Aguinaldo was enabled to collect taxes for the support of his revolutionary government from every native inhabitant of Manila, regardless of the fact that they were paying the regular taxes to the American authorities. Even the servants of the American officers and the men working in the company kitchens paid this tribute to Aguinaldo; and not only that, but many of these men were actually enrolled in the insurrectionary army, and used to work for the soldiers in the daytime and lie in the insurgent trenches at night, before the city was attacked.

Common Filipino Soldiers.
The bulk of the insurgent army, consisting of the militia class, wore no uniform whatever, but were dressed in the ordinary white clothing of the citizen. Probably two-thirds of the dead and wounded found on the field after a fight wore this white uniform. This facilitated their transition from soldiers to peaceable citizens, since all they had to do was to hide their guns or throw them into a river or slough. Even the uniformed soldiers carried a white suit in a little roll on their backs, and whenever they were in danger of being captured, they quickly changed their clothing and were transformed into "amigos." Many of them were captured with their clothing but half changed, while many of the dead upon the field were found provided with the white suit to be used for friendly purposes. Even the wounded undertook to change their clothing before falling into the Americans' hands. The orders which had been received by the American troops not to molest noncombatants partially accounted for this practice of the Filipinos carrying this white suit for use in emergencies, but it was learned from the Spaniards that it had always been the custom of the Filipinos to fight in bushwhacking style, representing themselves as friends whenever in danger of being captured. It was customary for the soldiers, when some stalwart young "amigo" in white clothes passed through the lines, to throw back his coat and examine his right shoulder, and frequently this was found to be black and blue, showing that he had been but recently repeatedly kicked by the butt of a gun, but "orders are orders," and they were allowed to pass through unmolested. All the scouting performed by Filipinos was done in white clothes and without arms, so that the Americans could not tell the scouts from other equally peaceable appearing citizens. They could go anywhere they chose without interference, even

Bato, the Filipino Stronghold in the Mountains of Bulucan Province near San Miguel. (See Page 37.)

within the American lines. On the other hand, American scouting parties had to go armed and in sufficient force to prevent themselves from being captured, and wherever they went their appearance was heralded by "amigos," who passed the word along and gave ample warning to all insurgents in the vicinity. Often the ladies of the family living in a hut by the wayside would be diligently engaged in serving out water to the thirsty soldiers, while the men of the family were equally as diligently engaged in scurrying through the brush to give the alarm of the approach of the dreaded "Americanos."

Mausers and Remingtons.

The Filipino army is now badly scattered, and but little of it is available for offensive operations. In each community the local forces are at hand for defense, but they are not in sufficient strength to make their defense formidable. The regular forces are scattered in the different districts under various leaders and cannot be concentrated for any serious offensive operations. Undoubtedly a great many of the 40,000 guns with which the insurrection was commenced have been lost by those who were compelled to throw them away for their own protection, while the bulk of the remainder are scattered about in this loosely organized body of soldiers. Were the leaders of the insurrection to agree to surrender their arms, it is doubtful if more than 5,000 or 6,000 could be turned in, the remainder being scattered all over the country in the hands of these guerrilla fighters. Comparatively few guns have fallen into our possession, and since the capture of the guns, rather than of the men, is the only guaranty of future peace, the outlook in this respect is not very encouraging. The offer of $30 Mexican each for rifles turned in by the natives has had little effect. The Mauser rifle, with which the Spanish army is armed and which constitutes the majority of the arms of the Filipinos, is a magazine gun holding five shells and having a caliber of 27 3/10, being even smaller than the 30 caliber Krag-Jorgensen rifle used by our regular army. Its range is somewhat longer than that of the Krag-Jorgensen, and much longer than the 45 caliber Springfield with which the volunteers were armed. The Mauser bullet is a small piece of lead encased in a steel jacket, which renders it very hard and enables it to pierce hard substances without being battered out of shape. It makes a round, smooth hole, even through bones, and does not mangle the flesh and break the bones like the larger, soft Springfield bullets. Thus the amputation of an arm or of a leg because of a wound from a Mauser is very rare, while the wounds from Springfield bullets render such amputations frequently necessary. The Remington used was of the same caliber as the Springfield. No. 45. The cartridge is a pointed lead

1—Utah Battery at La Loma Church in the Advance on Caloocan, February 10. 2—Kansans Repelling an Assault upon their Trenches at Caloocan. 3—The Burning of Paco Church, February 5, to Dislodge Sharpshooters. 4—A Filipino Battalion in Trenches.

slug encased in a brass jacket. Wounds from these brass covered bullets were apt to be poisoned by verdigris, and several cases of that kind occurred. If the brass casing was split when the bullet was fired the jagged ends made a horrible noise going through the air. A volunteer protested that the Filipinos were firing sewing machines and tin cans at him, and I heard one man say that these split brass bullets had whiskers and saw teeth. When the Filipinos ran short of ammunition for their Remingtons they saved the shells as they fired them and took them back to be reloaded. I have also seen a whole sackful of these empty shells captured and have also seen a great many of their reloaded cartridges. They also bought from Chinamen the empty shells of our own Springfields, which our authorities negligently permitted them to gather up after a battle. I have seen hundreds of these reloaded Springfield shells and have several in my possession. Their crude workmanship and the brand of our own manufacturers on the end easily identify them.

Volunteers with Springfields.
Most of the fighting during the spring campaign was done by the volunteers, who were kept constantly at the front, while the regular regiments sent out for reinforcements were for the most part kept in the city or along the inner line of defenses. This was because the volunteers were the best seasoned and the most experienced troops, the majority of the newly arrived regulars being recruits. The regulars were armed with Krag-Jorgensen magazine rifles, caliber No. 30, and used smokeless powder. The volunteers were armed with the old style, single fire Springfield rifle, caliber 45, and the bulk of the ammunition supplied them was black powder. There was issued a quantity of smokeless Springfield ammunition, but it was issued indiscriminately in connection with black powder, so that its smokeless effects were of little advantage. Just why the troops that were sent to the front were armed with this inferior weapon and compelled to use black powder, while a far superior weapon and smokeless powder were given to troops not in the field, is something the war department has never been able satisfactorily to explain. The explanations offered are too ridiculous for serious consideration, and the whole matter is another evidence of the thoughtless blundering and lack of care for the welfare of the troops which has marked the entire course of the Spanish war and the Filipino insurrection. Krag-Jorgensens were on hand and might have been issued to the volunteers had the commanding general desired to do so. They lay in boxes in San Francisco, long before they were sent to the island, and then lay in Manila without being issued to the troops. Finally in April a few were issued to each company, ostensibly for sharpshooting purposes, but the result of

A Portion of the Oregons Firing Volleys into Pasig to Cover the Advance of the Twentieth Regulars. (See Page 21.) Effects of Black Powder.

this was to complicate matters still more by making it necessary for each command to carry two styles of ammunition with which to supply the firing line.

Black Powder.

Even were there a possible excuse during this period of active campaigning for keeping the volunteers armed with Springfields, there can be none offered for not supplying them with smokeless powder. I have in my possession cartridges manufactured every year since 1876, which were issued to the volunteers, showing that all of the junk Springfield ammunition that could be bought or had accumulated in the arsenals was sent to the Philippines for the volunteers to use. I also have cartridges of black powder manufactured in June, 1898, two months after the Spanish war began, showing that even at that late date the ordnance department had not yet been aroused to the necessity of supplying the army with smokeless powder. The disadvantages of black powder are serious. The cloud of smoke exactly defines the position of the troops to the enemy, who can tell with accuracy where to direct their fire, while at the same time it so obscures the vision of those using it that they cannot aim effectively at the enemy. Troops using the smokeless powder always have a clear field of vision in front of them and are enabled to fire a number of volleys before their position can be detected by the enemy. For sharpshooting it is especially desirable, since it is extremely difficult to locate the position of a single sharpshooter using smokeless powder. The disadvantages of a Springfield rifle are its short range, its curved trajectory and the weight of the ammunition. Troops armed with it are at a great disadvantage in contending with troops armed with Mauser rifles. The Filipinos soon learned their advantage in this respect and always opened fire on our troops at long range. It was generally necessary for the volunteers to advance a long distance under fire before coming within effective range of their own weapon, and generally the Filipinos retreated as soon as this point was reached, selecting another position from which they could again do long range shooting. It was their treatment in the matter of arms and ammunition more than any other one thing, that so disgusted the volunteers that they wanted to quit the service, and few would reenlist, even with a bounty of $500 to $500 travel pay. The new United States Volunteers now being organized and sent to the Philippines are equipped with the Krag-Jorgensen rifle and smokeless powder, and they will not suffer from the disadvantage of having equipment inferior to that of the enemy. They are a fine body of men and worthy successors of those who carried on the war last spring in Luzon island.

The Third U. S. Artillery in the Trenches at Block House No. 2 in the Advance on Caloocan, February 10. (See Page 13.)

A Burial Party of the Wyomings near Santa Ana after the Battle of February 5.

Tree near Tinajeros from which Sharpshooters Fired into the Kansas, Montana and Third Artillery Trenches near Caloocan.

Filipino Sharpshooters.

On the opposite page is shown one of the tree perches used by the Filipino sharpshooters. This particular tree stands near the Tinajeros bridge, and was used by sharpshooters for firing into the Kansas and Montana trenches in front of Caloocan. Nearly every day somebody was hit by the numerous sharpshooters who kept pecking away at our trenches at extremely long range, and whose exact position could never be located because of their use of smokeless powder. Even had their position been known it would have been of little value to us, since they were careful to keep beyond the effective range of the Springfield rifle, although within good shooting distance with their own superior weapon. During the first fight of February 5, it was found that a great many sharpshooters were perched in the trees, where some of them remained even after our lines had passed by and fired upon our men from the rear. This was soon discovered and all trees were carefully inspected for a concealed enemy, and it became customary to fire small volleys into suspicious looking trees, so that many of these sharpshooters were killed and others were discouraged from following their example. After that very few sharpshooters remained in trees long enough for our own riflemen to get within good range of them. However, for the purpose of firing at our trenches at long range, and even for a better point from which to shoot at our advancing lines, these perches in the trees were still used, and many of them were observed as our lines passed along, but were invariably empty. Similar perches were made in the tops of tall banana trees, both for sharpshooting and for observation. In towns, also, little platforms were frequently constructed on the tops of houses, to be used for similar purposes.

Transportation.

The usual transportation in the field provided by the quartermaster's department was two wooden carts to each company, each drawn by a carabao bull (water buffalo), and driven by a Chinaman. This did not necessarily constitute the only transportation of the company, for I have seen companies with as many as six bull carts and two smaller carts, or caromatos, drawn by ponies, the additions having been procured in the ordinary way by levy upon the country for military purposes without authorization. Early in the spring 300 mules and a number of army wagons arrived from the United States, but these were used by the quartermaster's department in and around Manila, or were issued for company transportation to regular regiments stationed in the vicinity of the city, while the volunteer regiments that were doing the campaigning were still compelled to use the slow and aggravating bull teams. The rapidity of movement of the army at the front

Chinese Litter Bearers Accompanying the Hospital Corps at the Front.

was much retarded by this lack of adequate transportation; but it seems in keeping with the general policy that gave the fighting soldiers the short range gun and black powder, that they should also be given the tortoise-like bull team for transportation, while the mules and good army wagons were kept for use in the rear. Eight miles a day was almost the limit of progress of the bull team train. The carabaos required frequently to be refreshed with a bath in some stream or pond, and to be given a good rest. When pushed beyond their limit without this refreshment, I have seen them lie down and refuse to go further. I have also seen them work until they fell, completely exhausted, and die within a few minutes, and in less than half an hour puff up with gas like a balloon. An army with such transportation made but a sorry show in pursuing Filipinos, who were unhampered by impedimenta.

The water buffalo lives upon pallay, or unhulled rice, and common slough grass hay, and as both of these were easily obtainable wherever the army went, it was unnecessary to carry food for the animals. This constituted the only redeeming feature of bull transportation.

Chinese Litter Bearers. Whenever a command went into action, it was accompanied by a detachment of the hospital corps with stretchers for carrying the wounded from the field. Usually one member from the corps and one stretcher went with a company. At first enlisted men were detailed to carry these stretchers, but later Chinese litter bearers were employed, and, contrary to the usual opinion as to the courage and faithfulness of the Chinese, these men rendered most excellent service. I have seen these Chinamen go out behind the firing line under fire and bring in the wounded with as much courage and freedom from excitement as the hospital corps men who accompanied them. They seemed to be satisfied to go wherever the surgeon or his assistants were willing to lead them. Chinamen were also hired to drive the buffalo carts, on which rations and ammunition were carried with the column, but these Chinamen always exhibited a great deal of timidity when under fire, as they occasionally were, and the only reason I could ever give for this difference in conduct was the fact that one set of Chinamen had hired out as litter bearers, and did the work they were paid for doing, while the others did not put any bullets in their contract. I have been told that the Spanish army utilized Chinamen by the thousands for the transportation of supplies in the ordinary coolie fashion of carrying loaded baskets upon either end of a pole across the shoulder. My experience is that the Chinese were reliable and did whatever work they agreed to do with fidelity and energy.

Prisoners under Guard Bringing in a Wounded Filipino Soldier to an American Field Hospital.

Wounded Insurgents.

The treatment of wounded insurgents has been a matter much misunderstood in the United States and sadly misrepresented in many letters written home by thoughtless men. Owing to these letters many newspapers accused the soldiers of the Eighth Army Corps of violation of the rules of civilized warfare and of most savage and barbarous conduct, and not without reason, since from its own ranks came the letters upon which these slanders were based. They were accused of killing Filipinos in cold blood after they had been taken prisoners, and it was even asserted that this was done pursuant to orders from officers high in command. How untrue this is every soldier who has been on the firing line knows.

On the morning of February 5th, when the Americans drove the Filipinos from their intrenchments around Manila, there were several instances where wounded insurrectos lying on the ground attempted to shoot our soldiers after our line had passed. Several men were injured in this way, and there was one instance where a soldier was killed by an insurrecto who pretended to surrender. These instances being related throughout the army rendered the soldiers extremely angry, and many were heard to say that they would take no more chances with wounded Filipinos. This talk was heard among the line officers as well as the men, and in a few days it was rumored that orders had been given quietly not to take any more prisoners, and this was talked over so much among the men that, for a time, it was generally believed, though no soldier ever received such an order himself. By the time fighting was resumed six weeks later this vengeful spirit had considerably worn off. Undoubtedly, in the heat of action, some wounded Filipinos were shot or bayoneted as our lines rushed over captured intrenchments, but no instance has ever come to light where men once made prisoners were subsequently killed.

That prisoners were taken is shown by the fact that several thousand were under guard in Manila until the policy of letting all prisoners go was adopted, and that wounded were cared for is shown by the fact that several wards in the hospital at Manila were filled with Filipino wounded, who received the same surgical care and attention given our own men. I have seen too many wounded insurgents bandaged on the field by our soldiers as they passed over their lines, and carried to the rear by our hospital corps, to believe that the brave men who bore the brunt of battle in Luzon were not as humane and generous to a fallen foe, though a despised one, as brave men always are. They were the highest type of the American soldier and more than this cannot be said in praise of any man.

Sharpshooting from the California Trenches at San Pedro Macati. Filipino Stretcher in the Foreground. (See Page 55.)

A portion of the Washington Trenches at San Pedro Macati before the Capture of Guadelupe and Pasig.

Four Hundred Prisoners at Malapat ne Bato on their way to Manila, Captured in the Swamps around Pateros and Pasig by the Washingtons.

Filipino Prisoners.

During the first few weeks of the fighting, several thousand prisoners were taken and sent to Manila. Many of these were men actually captured with arms in their hands, but a majority of them were men found without arms in the immediate vicinity of the scene of the fight, and were believed to have been engaged in the conflict and to have hidden their arms for the purpose of representing themselves as non-combatants, or to have been in close sympathy with the insurrectos. Some were suspected of bushwhacking in the rear of our lines. The scene on the opposite page was one taken near the Pasig river, on the fifteenth of March, when 400 prisoners were sent in by the Washington regiment from the swamps in the vicinity of Pasig. These men were captured without arms, but all showed evidence of having had military training, and among them was a colonel of the Filipino army. Prisoners accumulated so fast in Manila, that the authorities finally released them all, on the theory that it was doing no good to keep them in confinement, and that they might become missionaries of peace when set at liberty, by telling their insurrecto friends how kind and tender-hearted the Americans were. Following out this same idea later in the campaign, prisoners captured in the field were kept a day or two, given a few square meals and permitted to go, with an injunction to tell their friends that the Americans were real good fellows; but it is doubtful if they did any more than to tell them that the Americans were fools. However, the mere capture of prisoners was of but little value when their arms were not secured, since Aguinaldo's army contained a great many more men than it did guns, yet it was gall and wormwood to the soldiers to see men captured in battle immediately turned loose again. It was especially galling to them to know that if these men were not actually soldiers themselves, they were freely through the lines, since they knew that if these men were not actually soldiers themselves, they were carrying information to the enemy, if not more substantial aid in the form of food.

The Black Hole of Santiago.

Fort Santiago occupies the northwest corner of the walled city fronting upon the river and bay, and it is especially designed as a protection to the city as against hostile approach by way of the river. Its armament consists chiefly of old-style bronze cannon manufactured from fifty to one hundred years ago, though a few more modern pieces are mounted there. It was over this fort that the official garrison flag was raised, as a formal act of taking possession of the city, on the afternoon of August 13, by Lieutenant Brumby, representing the navy, and Lieutenant Povey, of the Second Oregon, representing the army, with a special guard of honor composed of Company A of the Second Oregon. The chief interest in the fort, however,

77

Fort Santiago, Manila, near Mouth of Pasig River, Garrisoned by the Twenty-third Regulars.

Interior of Paco Cemetery, showing Graves of Soldiers, also Burial Niches in the Wall.

Writing Letters on the Firing Line, a Scene in the Montana Trenches.

rests in what is known as the black hole, a dungeon in the stone wall partially below the level of the water. In this it was customary for the Spaniards to keep Filipino prisoners. It is related that during the insurrection of 1897 this dungeon was filled with Filipino suspects, and that one night they were all suffocated to death because of the failure of the guard to open the air-hole; and this failure is believed by the Filipinos to have been the result of design, rather than of carelessness. This fort has been occupied almost continuously by the Twenty-third Infantry as a portion of the provost guard. Salutes are fired from it in returning salutes of visiting warships of foreign nations.

Writing Home.

The scene on the opposite page of the Montana boys in their trenches writing letters to their friends and relatives at home is one that could have been witnessed almost daily along the lines of the regiments at the front, especially on days immediately before the sailing of the transports. The dispatch of mail to the United States was a very uncertain matter. For some reason best known to itself, the quartermaster's department refused to give any information as to the sailing dates of transports until they were actually loaded and under orders to sail. The postoffice was then notified, and wherever possible the obliging superintendent of the postal department, Mr. Vaille, sent word by telephone or otherwise to the various regimental headquarters. This left but a few hours at the most in which the soldiers might write letters for home. Much dissatisfaction existed throughout the army because of this discourtesy of the quartermaster's department.

Sometimes paper and envelopes were a scarce article in the trenches, and men frequently tore off the sides of paper cartridge boxes and wrote letters on them, putting the address and the stamp on the opposite side and mailing them as they would a postal card. Frequently, also, envelopes were woven out of bamboo or palm leaf strips and letters inclosed in them. No doubt these odd letters and envelopes will be cherished as great souvenirs of the campaign by those who received them. Mail from home was received about once in three weeks, and its arrival always created great excitement in the camp. From one end to the other the cry of "mail, mail!" was shouted, and there was a great rush to the point of distribution. Generally the chaplain of each regiment acted as postmaster for the command, keeping on hand a supply of stamps and stationery and maintaining practically a branch postoffice. For a day or two after the receipt of mail the quarters were full of men reading the newspapers and trying to keep posted on what was going on at home, then the usual routine would be resumed until another mail day.

81

The Colorados Pitching Shelter Tents preparatory to going into Camp.

Military Cemeteries.

The Americans who died at Cavite, prior to the capitulation of Manila, were buried in a tract set aside for that purpose on the Marine Hospital grounds. It was low and unsuited for this purpose, and its use was discontinued as soon as possible. After the surrender of Manila, the regular cemetery at Paco, a southeastern suburb of the city, was used for this purpose. This cemetery is a circular tract about 200 feet in diameter and inclosed by two concentric cement walls about 30 feet apart and about 12 feet high. Facing inward are three tiers of niches running clear around each inclosing wall, each niche being large enough to receive a coffin. Bodies inclosed in coffins are placed in these niches, the front of which is then cemented up and faced with a memorial tablet. Some of the deceased soldiers were interred in these niches, while others were buried in the ground, according to the American custom, in the tract within the walls.

After the attack upon Manila, when the Filipinos had been driven away from the immediate vicinity of the city, a special army cemetery was established on Artillery Knoll, between Paco and Santa Ana. Here most of those who were killed in battle were buried, each grave being carefully numbered and registered and provided with a substantial wooden headboard. On Memorial Day services were held in both of the cemeteries, and all the graves were profusely decorated with flowers, each company and special corps in the army attending to the decoration of the graves of its fallen members. The war department declared its intention last spring to send all the bodies of deceased soldiers back to the United States to be delivered free to their friends, if they desired, or to be buried at the government's expense in a national cemetery. A start was made on this work at that time, but it was found that it would not be practicable to move the bodies for at least six months, so that it is probable that this work will not be undertaken until next winter.

Pitching Shelter Tents.

In Manila most of the troops were quartered in the barracks formerly occupied by the Spanish soldiers, and in other large buildings taken for that purpose, yet some of them, especially those near the outskirts of the city, were in tents, known as "shelter tents," sometimes called "dog tents," and generally referred to by the soldiers as "pup tents." These tents are in the form of the letter A with the apex about five feet from the ground. One tent accommodates two men, and on the march each man carries one shelter half, with his proportion of the poles necessary for pitching the tent. When the command goes into camp each company lines up at a proportional distance between the men, and each couple pitches its own tent. Generally these tents were pitched in the open rice fields, and it not infrequently occurred that heavy rains in the

84

Santolan Pumping Station for Manila Water System at San Mateo River, showing Marquina Valley in the Background. This was Captured by the Nebraskas and Held by Them and the Coloradoes.

night would drown the soldiers out, the rice ridges containing the water so that it rose rapidly. Because of this, wherever it was possible, the men were quartered in the native huts, where they could keep dry and were much more comfortable. The Filipino troops lived entirely in these huts, having no tentage. On the campaign, the men at first carried a shelter half, a blanket and a poncho; but towards the end most of them left the blanket behind, and covered themselves only with their ponchos. During the siege of Manila, in the rainy season of 1898, little platforms were built a foot or two above the ground, and shelter tents pitched upon these in order to keep out of the water and mud, and this practice was adopted again when the rainy season began in the present year wherever troops were compelled to live in tents. A shelter tent is a veritable sweat-house in the daytime under the heating rays of a tropical sun, and whenever possible the men always constructed some more satisfactory shelter to protect them from the sun.

Manila Water Works.
One of the most strategic positions held by the American troops was the water-works which supplied Manila with fresh water. This system consists of a pumping station on the San Mateo river at Santolan, underground reservoirs midway between Santolan and the city, known as the "deposito," and a large iron pipe line running from the pumping station to the deposito and thence to the city. During the American occupation of Manila, prior to the capitulation, both the deposito and pumping station were in the hands of the Filipinos. They had cut off the supply of water from the Spanish during the siege of Manila, but it had been turned on again after the surrender of the city. It was determined immediately to capture these positions from the Filipinos, and this was done on the second day of the fight by the Nebraska regiment and the third battalion of the Tennessees and the third battalion of the Oregons, who drove the Filipinos steadily until they had possession of the entire ground covered by the water system. The Nebraskas were then stationed at Santolan and along the pipe line towards the city, and the Oregons near the "deposito." For more than a month these troops had almost daily and nightly conflicts with the enemy. When the advance on Malolos was made, the Colorados relieved the Nebraskas at the pumping station and held it until June, having frequent conflicts with the enemy, who annoyed them by persistent attacks during the night time.

The water is not of the best quality, and by orders it was all boiled for drinking purposes, each company boiling its own water and keeping it in barrels for company use. An army distilling plant was set up

Company Mess in the Field.

early in the spring, and distilled water was furnished to the troops in the field, whenever practicable, either by sending it up the Pasig river on boats, or out along the line of the railroad on cars. In the field occasionally good water could be found in wells and springs and in running streams above the influence of the tides, but even in the field water was generally boiled before drinking. Much of the sickness in the army when Manila was first occupied was due to the difficulty of compelling the men to drink the boiled water at times when they were not under the observation of their officers. Most of the companies constructed large charcoal filters in wine barrels and kept ice in the boiled and filtered water.

Company Mess.

The messing of troops, whether in field or garrison, was done entirely by companies. Only on board the transports, where facilities were not provided for company messes, was the cooking done for larger bodies. The cooking utensils issued by the government for use in the Philippines were what is known as Buzzycott ovens, with an assortment of pots and pans, a large coffee boiler and various smaller utensils. As a rule a hole was dug in the ground for the fireplace and the irons upon which the oven rested were placed over it. The cooking was done by enlisted men, detailed for that purpose, who were usually paid extra by a small monthly contribution by each member of the company, or received a portion of the company fund provided for in the regulations. The assistants in the kitchen, known as the kitchen police, were detailed regularly by roster or were given this work as a punishment for breaches of discipline. Many of the companies hired Spanish prisoners or Filipinos to work in the kitchen. Regular mess-call was sounded by the musician of the guard three times a day, and each company lined up at its own company kitchen. The men were served in turn by the kitchen assistants, each man having his own mest ration can, tin cup, knife, fork and spoon. After receiving his allowance, he selected the most comfortable place on the ground or adjacent rice paddy and ate his meal. As a usual thing there were "seconds" on most of the articles on the bill of fare, so that those who did not have enough at the first helping could fall in line again for more.

The chief components of the army ration are fresh meat and fresh bread, when practicable, bacon, canned salmon, beans, rice, hard bread, potatoes, onions, coffee and sugar. It is the privilege of the company to commute portions of these rations into cash and use the money for the purpose of buying other things to eat, and many companies thus traded rations to the value of $100 a month, thus making the bill of fare much more complete and agreeable.

The Ayuntemiunto, known as "The Palace," in the Walled City, Headquarters of the Department of the Pacific and Eighth Army Corps.

The general headquarters of the Department of the Pacific and the Eighth Army are maintained in a large threestory building on Cabildo street in the walled city, generally called by the Americans "The Palace." This building was, in fact, the Ayuntamiento, or general city government building. It was here that General Merritt first raised his flag and established his headquarters when he took possession of Manila. On the lower floor of this building are quartered the special headquarters of the guard and a company of bombers of the fire department. Here, also, are stables for horses used by the officials. On the second floor is a large council chamber, on whose walls are hung pictures of Magellan and other men prominent in the history of the islands. This room is now used by the paymasters. On this floor, also, is the government printing office. On the third floor are the offices of the commanding general, adjutant general, the chief quartermaster, chief paymaster, chief surgeon, chief signal officer and chief engineer, also a courtroom used by the military tribunal and the office of the judge advocate general.

Lawton's Scouts.

When Lawton started north on his expedition to San Isidro, W. H. Young, a civilian of much experience in Indian warfare, offered to organize a select band of scouts for the purpose of scouring the country and fighting the Filipinos in their own style, by bushwhacking. His offer was accepted, and he organized a band of twenty-six from the North Dakota, Oregon and Fourth Cavalry regiments. For a month they ranged over the country in advance of the main column, and many a Filipino outpost was driven in or annihilated, until the insurgents began to have a panicky feeling in regard to the Americans who fired upon them from such unexpected quarters and seemed to be ubiquitous and devoid of fear. The most brilliant work of the scouts was the capture of San Ildefonso and San Miguel and the route of the Filipinos at the burning of Tarbon bridge. For more than a week Summers' brigade had remained in front of a strong position held by 1500 insurgents at San Ildefonso, five miles from San Miguel, the most important town in that region next to San Isidro, waiting for orders to advance. One morning before Jaylight Young started out with his scouts to feel the enemy's position and soon he had a battle royal started. The entire Filipino force began shooting in volleys and rapid fire along their whole front in response to the sharpshooting of the scouts, and they kept this up for several hours until their nerves could stand no longer the tension of being fired upon by an unseen foe. Then they abandoned their position and retreated to San Miguel. The scouts followed, supported by two companies of the Minnesotas and Oregons, and in the same way drove them out of the

Capture of the Burning Bridge at Tarlac by Lawton's Scouts.

town. That night the forces of General Summers occupied both places without having fired a shot besides the bushwhacking fire of the scouts. One man was slightly wounded at San Ildefonso and Young himself was severely wounded at San Miguel, dying the next day at the hospital in Manila, whither he was sent with all haste.

After the death of Young, Lieutenant J. E. Thornton, of the Oregons, was given command of the scouts, and under him they continued their good work. It was only a few days later they achieved their most brilliant feat. Near San Isidro there is a narrow but unfordable river, with high, precipitous banks, and this is crossed at Tarbon by a wooden bridge, which was heavily defended by intrenchments on the opposite side of the stream. When Pilar retired into San Isidro he left 200 of his best troops of the Manila regiment to defend the bridge, with orders to burn it if they could not hold it. When Thornton with 20 men arrived within sight of the structure it was on fire. The main column was a mile behind him and he had no time to wait for it if the bridge was to be saved for the crossing of the army. He promptly deployed his 20 men and began a rapid, but stealthy advance through the tall swamp grass. The men kept a general alignment at an interval of about 100 feet, and began sharpshooting at every head they saw appear above the trenches. In this way they worked themselves up to the opposite side of the stream and had the enemy so terrorized that but a few of them had courage enough to poke their heads up far enough to get a good shot. Suddenly Thornton and three others rushed across the burning bridge and began shooting along the flank and rear of the trenches. Then came the panic. The insurgents might have rushed upon the daring men and killed them, but instead of doing so, the whole 200 took to their heels and sought safety in the high grass back of the river, while the scouts stood there and shot them as long as there was one in sight. Six dead and seven wounded were found on the ground, and 26 wounded were heard of the next day at San Isidro. One scout was killed, an Oregonian named Harrington, of whom Lawton said his death was equal to the loss of a whole battalion.

1.—Caloocan Railroad Station, used as a Field Hospital during the Battle of Malabon, March 25. 2.—Tenajeros Bridge, Showing Span Destroyed to Prevent the Crossing of Wheaton's Brigade at the Battle of Malabon. 3.—Malabon Bridge, Showing Span Destroyed to Prevent Americans from Entering the City. 4.—General Wheaton and the Firing Line of the Third and Twenty-second Regulars and One Gun of the Utah Battery at Malinta, March 26. 5.—Kansans Fording Bag Bag River in the Advance upon Calumpit.

www.ingramcontent.com/pod-product-compliance
Lightning Source LLC
Chambersburg PA
CBHW020256090426
42735CB00009B/1098